EARTH

MURRAY "OAK" TAPETA

OUTER SPACE

NORWOOD HOUSE PRESS

Cataloging-in-Publication Data

Names: Tapeta, Murray.
Title: Earth / Murray Tapeta.
Description: Buffalo, NY : Norwood House Press, 2026. | Series: Outer space | Includes glossary and index.
Identifiers: ISBN 9781978574779 (pbk.) | ISBN 9781978574786 (library bound) | ISBN 9781978574793 (ebook)
Subjects: LCSH: Earth (Planet)--Juvenile literature.
Classification: LCC QB631.4 T374 2026 | DDC 525--dc23

Published in 2026 by
Norwood House Press
2544 Clinton Street
Buffalo, NY 14224

Copyright © 2026 Norwood House Press
Designer: Rhea Magaro
Editor: Kim Thompson

Photo credits: Cover, p. 1 GizemG/Shutterstock.com; pp. 5, 7, 11 NASA; p. 6 Aphelleon/Shutterstock.com; p. 9 JLStock/Shutterstock.com; p. 10 Dusya Kan/Shutterstock.com; pp. 12, 13 Herschel Hoffmeyer/Shutterstock.com; p. 15 Porstocker, Allexxandar/Shutterstock.com; p. 16 leeborn/Shutterstock.com; p. 17 Shestak Vera/Shutterstock.com; p. 18 Kletr; p. 21 Andrei Armiagov/Shutterstock.com

All rights reserved. No part of this book may be reproduced in any form without permission in writing from the publisher, except by a reviewer.

Printed in the United States of America

Some of the images in this book illustrate individuals who are models. The depictions do not imply actual situations or events.

CPSIA compliance information: Batch #CSNHP26: For further information contact Norwood House Press at 1-800-237-9932.

TABLE OF CONTENTS

Where Is Earth? 4

Earth's Moon 8

Planet Earth 10

Amazing Earth 14

Exploring Earth 20

Glossary 22

Thinking Questions 23

Index 24

About the Author 24

Where Is Earth?

Our **solar system** has eight planets. Earth is the third planet from the Sun. It is a little bigger than its neighbor Venus.

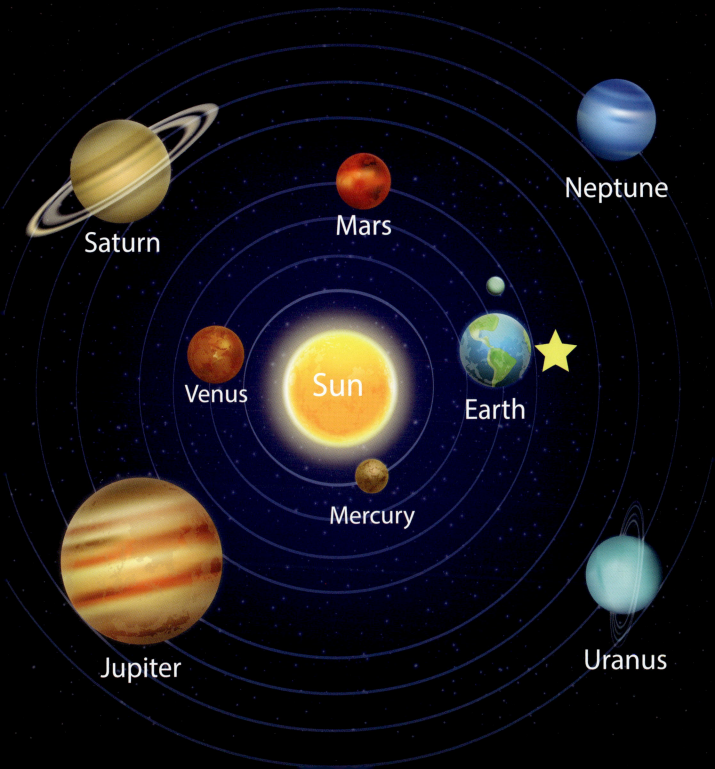

Earth is about 93 million miles (149 million kilometers) away from the Sun. It is just the right distance to support life.

One year on Earth is 365 days long. It takes Earth that long to **orbit** the Sun.

Earth's Moon

Earth is the only planet in our solar system with just one moon. Earth's moon orbits Earth. We can see it because it reflects light from the Sun.

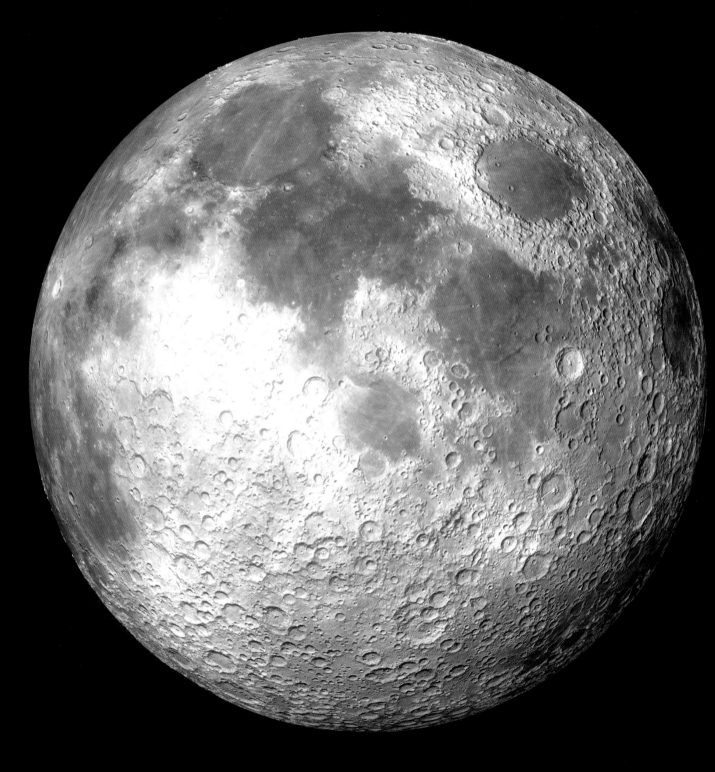

Planet Earth

Earth is a **terrestrial** planet. Its surface is firm and rocky.

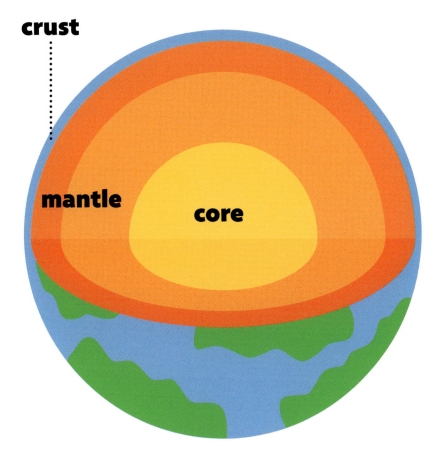

Planet Earth has three layers. The crust is the outer layer where living things are found. Below the crust is a **mantle** made of solid and molten rock. Earth's **core** is super-hot metal.

Scientists think Earth began nearly five billion years ago. It was a large spinning disk of dust and gas. Over time, a planet formed.

Earth has gone through many changes. Billions of years after Earth formed, dinosaurs began to stomp around. Millions of years later, humans appeared.

Amazing Earth

There is no other known planet like Earth. Liquid water has not been found on the surfaces of other planets in our solar system. It covers nearly three-quarters of Earth. All that water makes Earth look blue-green from space. Earth is called "the blue planet."

Earth is surrounded by an **atmosphere**. This thick layer of gases provides the air we breathe. It is mostly **nitrogen** and **oxygen**.

Earth's atmosphere protects the planet. It blocks harmful rays from the Sun. It also traps heat from the Sun so that the planet stays warm enough for life.

Heat, water, and other resources make life on Earth possible. Millions of plant and animal **species** live on Earth. Life has not been found on any other planet.

Exploring Earth

Satellites are sent by scientists to explore other planets. They explore Earth too! Over 25,000 satellites orbit Earth. They take photos. They do experiments. They collect data about forests, oceans, weather patterns, and more.

Glossary

atmosphere (AT-muhs-feer): the mixture of gases that surrounds a planet; air

core (kor): most inner part; center

mantle (MAN-tuhl): the part of Earth between the crust and the core which is made of solid and molten rock

nitrogen (NYE-truh-juhn): a colorless, odorless gas which makes up about four-fifths of Earth's atmosphere

orbit (OR-bit): to follow a curved path around a larger body in space

oxygen (AHK-si-juhn): a colorless gas which is found in air and water and which animals need to breathe

satellites (SAT-uh-lites): spacecrafts sent into orbit around a planet, moon, or other object in space

solar system (SOH-lur SIS-tuhm): the Sun and everything that orbits around it

species (SPEE-seez): types of plants and animals

terrestrial (tuh-RES-tree-uhl): made up of rocks or metals and having a hard surface

Thinking Questions

1. Why is Earth able to support life?

2. Why does Earth appear blue-green from space?

3. How do scientists think Earth formed?

4. What are the three layers of planet Earth?

5. How do satellites explore Earth?

Index

atmosphere 16, 17

changes 13

layers 11

living things 6, 11, 13, 17, 19

moon 8

orbit 7, 8, 20

satellites 20

solar system 4, 8, 14

Sun 4, 6–8, 17

water 14, 19

About the Author

Murray "Oak" Tapeta was born in a cabin without plumbing in Montana. Growing up in the great outdoors, he became a lover of nature. He earned the nickname "Oak" after climbing to the top of an oak tree at the age of three. Oak loves to read and write. He has written many books about events in history and other subjects that fascinate him. He prefers spending time in the wilderness with his dog Birchy.